T0385104

Madame
TUSSAUD

WHO WAS...

Madame TUSSAUD

Waxwork Queen of the French Revolution

TONY THORNE

✳ SHORT BOOKS

Published in 2004 by
Short Books
15 Highbury Terrace
London N5 1UP

10 9 8 7 6 5 4 3 2

A CIP catalogue record for this book
is available from the British Library.

ISBN 1-904095-85-2

Printed in Great Britain by
Bookmarque Ltd, Croydon, Surrey

For Eddie

Every day of the year, big red double-decker buses crammed with tourists and visitors from out of town crawl slowly in the heavy traffic along the Marylebone Road, in London. And every day the passengers on the top deck look down, nudge one another and wonder out loud what that long, long line of people is that snakes for hundreds of metres along the pavement below them, starting in a distant side street, standing still for ages, then filing very slowly beneath the roadside plane trees and sycamores, to disappear finally through a wide, dark doorway.

The conductor, the driver and the other Londoners

on board know where the line is going and what lies behind the glass doors: a magical place where ordinary people can come to gaze at the superstars and celebrities – sports personalities, top models, actors, musicians – of the 21st century, and wander among the legendary heroes, heroines and villains of times past. Londoners know that this is the queue for Madame Tussaud's exhibition of waxwork wonders, but few even of them know how this first, great London exhibition came to be there, or how it came by its curious, French-sounding name.

The story of Tussaud's, its models and the waxworker who fashioned them is a long and colourful one, and began in an older, very different world…

SHIPWRECKED

As the *Earl Moira* battled the heavy seas on its crossing from Liverpool to Dublin, the passengers, huddled shivering below, grew more and more afraid for their lives. The crew were nowhere to be found, and no one else dared venture in the pitch dark across the deck – lashed again and again by huge waves and driving rain – to see if the captain was still at the wheel. If they had, it would have done them little good: the man had been hopelessly drunk when they set off and a short time before, as the little ship lurched into Irish waters, the heaving black sea had swept him off into the night.

Of the one hundred travellers who cowered in the

darkness only half would see dry land again. We cannot know what they were thinking, each lost in fearful silence, deafened by the storm, but one among them, a small elderly lady wrapped in a thick woollen cloak under a borrowed greatcoat, must have felt a familiar surge of terror, a sensation that brought with it a jumble of unwelcome, half-buried memories of other dark places and frightened faces.

The *Earl Moira* wallowed helplessly in the surging seas, then, with a terrible grinding groan, its hull struck a hidden sandbank. Astonishingly, the whole vessel became still for an instant, frozen in the churning water and quite silent. The main mast very, very slowly toppled sideways and as it hit the deck a host of other unearthly noises – the screeching of twisting iron rails, the rumble of barrels broken free, the deep creaking and cracking of splitting timbers – accompanied the thunderous crash. The ship's bows disappeared beneath the waterline, the upper deck slid into the sea as the hull began to come apart. Now there were other faint sounds – gasps and screams, as darting figures appeared from all around the crazily tilting main deck, slithering and scampering and splashing through the wash, dodging the iron girders and wooden chests which swept past them, all making for the only one of the ship's lifeboats that was still hanging in its cradle.

***

In the pale light of a damp early morning the same grey-haired lady, still enveloped in her soaking cloak and stiffening, creaking crinolines, rapped on the weather-beaten door of a seafront cottage, waking the astonished fisherman and his wife, who peered out bleary-eyed.

'Where are we? Is this Ireland?' The lady's voice was firm but the accent was heavily foreign.

'Tis Worden, near Preston – in Lancashire, England.'

'You must help us,' the little lady ordered, 'we have been shipwrecked, we are cold and hungry.'

A bedraggled young man who was standing behind

her stepped forward. 'Our party has been in the water all night, until first light when we came upon the beach. We would most appreciate your assistance.'

The fisherman looked puzzled. 'But if you reached land at dawn, where have you been since then?'

The foreign lady looked levelly at the fisherman. 'Searching the shoreline for my models. They are lost, all lost.'

***

The little French lady with the long nose and the silver spectacles found lodgings in a grand house further up the coast, and spent a few days there recovering from her ordeal. All her heavy trunks were at the bottom of the sea, but by a miracle her models – a set of little dolls made of wax with the features of famous historical figures – were washed up on the shore a few days later and brought to the house, where she was carefully calculating her losses in a ledger.

The daughters of the family, Mary Hannah and

Susan, peered through the half-open door of the study at the models laid out on a table. Their yellowish bodies were naked but smooth and featureless where the signs of maleness or femaleness should have been. (The girls giggled, nervous but secretly disappointed.)

The models' faces, though, were wonderfully lifelike – much more delicate and detailed than even the most expensive dolls – and the salt water seemed to have done the hard wax no damage. The girls had time to notice a plump gentleman with a proud expression, a lady with a high forehead and a rosebud mouth, an old man who seemed to be asleep – or was he perhaps... dead?

The family were intrigued by the brisk little Frenchwoman. At dinner she told them that she was the owner of a travelling wax museum, and that from the little statuettes they had seen she could make life-size figures to exhibit to the public.

So this was the famous Madame Tussaud herself!

As a parting gift, the lady of the house, Mrs Ffarington, gave her unexpected guest a selection of beautiful antique clothes from their wardrobes. 'Please take these, Madame, to replace the costumes you have lost.'

CHAPTER ONE

It was in Strasbourg, a medieval city of dark towers, immense tiled roofs and stone bridges that sits on the broad river Rhine where France and Germany meet, that in 1760 a girl called Anna Maria was born. Her father, Joseph Grosholtz, was one of the bravest soldiers in the army of Count Dagobert Würmser which fought in the Seven Years' War that ebbed back and forth across Europe and its empires in the middle of the 18th century.

Before he got his wounds, (so the story goes) the young officer, Joseph Grosholtz of Frankfurt, had been a handsome man. One day on leave in Strasbourg, in a garden on the riverside, he had met a plump and cheerful teenage girl named Anna Maria Walder and they had fallen in love and got married. Joseph then returned to the wars, but in a battle not long afterwards his forehead had been laid open to the bone, leaving a huge livid scar that never truly healed. In another, his lower jaw had been shot clean away. Surgeons patched up the wounds as best they could and where the hero's mouth had been they wedged a silver plate shaped roughly like a man's chin. Back in Strasbourg, the citizens hid their horror and turned and nodded respectfully when Grosholtz walked by, leaning on the arm of his young wife.

The years of fighting ruined Joseph's health and in the autumn of 1760, on one of his rare visits, his heart stopped and his eyes glazed over and he fell down dead on the cobbled street. Two months later his widow gave birth to a daughter who was given the same name as her mother. Not long afterwards the older Anna Maria took the younger with her to Berne in Switzerland, where she had arranged to work as housekeeper for a doctor, Philippe Kreutzer, whose family preferred to be known by the more distinguished Latin name of Curtius. Little Anna Maria was told to call the doctor 'uncle', while he treated her as if she was his own child. Curtius's neighbours in Berne were forever curious about his new housekeeper. They could never decide whether she was his cousin, as he sometimes said, or just a family friend – or was she really a sister that the family was ashamed of? And if so, was the quiet little girl really his niece or… no one has ever been sure.

The most brilliant student of his generation, Curtius had been destined for a career in medicine, and had started to work as a doctor before he was twenty years old. But Curtius nursed a secret that, if shared, would ruin for ever his chances of becoming a famous physician. He had never been able to stand the sight of blood – if he had to dissect a corpse as part of his studies, or cut open the body of a gravely ill patient, he would start to vomit uncontrollably or fall down in a faint. What Curtius preferred to do was work on the lifelike wax models which the medical profession used in those days to learn about the human body when the real thing was not available. He even started to make model parts himself – arms, legs and internal organs – moulding them and painting them with a skill that astonished everyone who saw them.

Modelling was not only less terrifying than treating living patients, the ambitious young man quickly realised that it could also make him money. He began to sculpt portraits of local celebrities and then started making statues of famous figures from history and literature. Soon the Curtius home became a gallery where rich customers could come and view the marvels on display. For his favourite clients, Curtius made comical and rude figures to be passed around and sniggered over in secret.

One of the distinguished visitors to the house in Berne was the Prince de Conti, who was so impressed that he invited the brilliant young artist-doctor to return with him to Paris, the wealthiest and most glamorous city in Europe, where he promised to introduce him to his cousin, the King of France. Curtius accepted immediately, told Anna Maria and her mother to look after the household while he was gone and galloped off after his new protector. In Paris the Prince provided an apartment and servants and the doctor set to work. During the long months that followed Anna Maria's mother read aloud to her the short, breathless letters from her uncle. His energies were all spent on fashioning his models, on supervising his workmen and flattering his clients.

After two years Curtius' studio had become the most stylish attraction in that style-conscious city. He bought an imposing house where he entertained lords and ladies, poets and playwrights; the celebrated and the powerful. And now that he was quite sure that Paris was going to be his home he sent for his housekeeper and her daughter to help him run his new household and the booming business. For five days Anna Maria, her mother and her maiden aunt who had joined them from Strasbourg bounced on their hard seats as their carriage swayed and bumped along the country roads to their new home at number 20, Boulevard du Temple.

***

At first little Anna Maria was frightened to leave her mother's side – the bustling city around them was nothing like dull, respectable Berne or sleepy Strasbourg: so noisy – and the French that everyone spoke was just a babble to her ears. But her uncle's coachman and the old man who tended the garden and the flower-sellers in the street outside all spoke kindly and slowly to her and little by little she began to understand what they were saying.

'Anna Maria is not a French name,' they declared, 'We will call you Marie.' Soon Marie could speak the language fluently herself. She loved to watch her mother and aunt cooking up Strasbourg sausages and sour cabbage in the steaming kitchen, and she loved to mingle with the customers who crowded into the waxworks museum, even on Sundays when they should have been at church.

Curtius never stopped working to satisfy his customers' thirst for novelties. As well as Egyptian pharaohs, Greek gods and goddesses and Roman emperors in their silver and gold finery, his hall in the smart Palais Royal district had war heroes, famous actors, and freaks – like the world's fattest man and the girl who had slept for a hundred years. Musicians played sad or dramatic music from behind a screen and a hidden ventriloquist made the figures themselves seem to speak.

At home in the Boulevard du Temple, Marie was introduced to aristocrats from all over Europe and some of the most famous politicians of the time. She met Lafayette, the French Marquis (nobleman) who fought in the American War of Independence, and Benjamin Franklin, the American statesman. And, at the head of the dinner table, leading the conversation or in the middle of a chattering crowd in the ballroom, there was always her uncle. The popular Dr Curtius was a strange character and Marie was never sure if she really knew him at all. Nor was she sure whether she could really *like* him, even if she would always be grateful to him for giving her a home and taking charge of her education. He was a restless man, never still, always intriguing, a shrewd and ruthless businessman, charming and flattering when it suited him, keeping whatever his private thoughts and feelings were to himself. In his thin, grey face were set two wild eyes that glinted and glared.

When Marie was only six years old, her uncle began to teach her to sculpt in clay. He was the strictest of teachers, but Marie showed a natural skill for modelling and for drawing from life which was the equal of uncle Philippe's. Before long the little girl could even help with the most delicate tasks, like placing the individual hairs in the head of a wax portrait.

Marie was sent to study the cutting and sewing of the costumes with her uncle's assistants. His carpenters showed her how the wooden stands and wire frames inside the models were fastened together and bent into shape, but it was Curtius himself who sat with her and showed her how to draw the knife through the clay and to use her fingers to squeeze out the form of a cheek or a chin.

As she carefully painted on the features with a fine-haired brush, she sometimes turned to see her uncle gaping for a second in admiration, before he caught himself and began to frown again. He was the only one who recognised the special gift she had – the ability to read a person's character in the curl of a lip, the lifting of an eyebrow, and then to capture it in a stroke of the knife or the brush. Her eye for detail was remarkable: many years later she could still recall the exact colour of the slippers that an actress wore, the number of buttons on an ambassador's waistcoat.

When she was sixteen Curtius allowed Marie to sculpt the heads of two of his most distinguished dinner guests, the great writers and thinkers Jean-Jacques Rousseau and François-Marie Voltaire, and he proudly displayed the busts in his new and even more splendid exhibition, the *Cabinet de Cire*. Marie's own reputation as a waxworker was beginning to grow.

CHAPTER TWO

One morning Dr Curtius called Marie excitedly into his study. Wedging himself behind the enormous carved desk, he leaned forward out of his plush-and-mahogany chair and roared at her, just as if she were a crowd of spectators and not alone in the big book-lined room, just a few feet from him.

'My child, Marie, my dear child,' he rasped, 'I have the most wonderful news for you – indeed, for both of us, and for all our family...' At first Marie was too distracted by the lifesize, and very lifelike head of Voltaire, the head which she herself had moulded and which sat on the desk at exactly the same height as her uncle's. For a moment it seemed as if both men

– the agitated showman-doctor and the thin-lipped, quizzical philosopher – were glaring at her across the polished tabletop. 'My dining and entertaining, my pulling of strings, my clever and careful cultivation of my friends at court has been successful. I have secured for you employment at Versailles, in the royal household no less! You are to teach the arts of drawing and sculpture to the King's sister, Madame Elisabeth, and then, when they are old enough, to the royal children. They will require of you, too, that you sketch and paint scenes of their life for their amusement, and I have asked that, if they are pleased with your work, you be allowed to exercise your genius and model their majesties themselves for public exhibition.'

Marie was from a humble background, just a shrewd, plain-speaking Swiss girl. She was twenty years old now – an age at which many young women were already married – but she had no time for girlish things. Flirtation, small talk and tittle-tattle bored her so that often people thought her rather prim and severe.

'Mademoiselle Marie is married to her work,' the

servants said. She had been a brilliant student of drawing and model-making, but she had learnt other lessons in her uncle's household, too. She knew when to speak and when to listen and watch and say nothing. Her manners were perfect and if she really had to, she could recite poems or passages from the Bible as well as any well brought-up young lady. She was properly respectful, but never overawed by the aristocrats and artists and musicians to whom she was regularly presented by her uncle.

In her dreams she sometimes found herself living among these people, a famous and talented woman, surrounded by admirers and waited on by teams of servants, but once she was awake again, she felt relieved to be watching quietly from the sidelines, pouring all her energy and feelings into her own creation, her world of models. The girl who had sculpted Rousseau and Voltaire felt only a tiny twinge of alarm at the thought of meeting the King and Queen of France.

Her mother and aunt had taught her the strict rules of polite society: the wife of a lawyer must be known as

'Mademoiselle', the wife of a courtier as 'Madame'; a doctor was a gentleman, a surgeon could never be more than a mere citizen. But inside the vast palace at Versailles, where line upon line of *valets de chambre*, footmen, maids in waiting, maids of honour, ladies of the chamber, ladies of the wardrobe, keepers of the seal, bearers of the seal, lackeys, lickspittles and lordlings, ministers, marquis and marquises, comtes and comtesses, duchesses, dukes, princesses, prince-lings, princes-of-the-blood and princes-of-the-line advanced and withdrew through tier upon tier of ante-rooms, dressing-rooms, bedchambers, drawing-rooms and ballrooms, the rules of behaviour for life at court were far more complicated. Marie was presented with a leather-bound manual containing five hundred pages of courtly regulations, titles and forms of address, and told to learn it by heart within the week.

At the time that Marie moved to Versailles, France was in a state of turmoil. The country was short of food and fuel, and the people were beginning to protest about the hardship of their lives. As she studied the fat book by candlelight, Marie thought to herself that just a few yards from her uncle's door, and a few steps beyond the railings that surrounded the palace at Versailles, barefoot and filthy children dressed in rags were begging for pieces of bread that now cost more than a week's wages. The thought that she was living in luxury while they were starving niggled and worried her. But it was a thought that she had to hide away for the moment, while she concentrated on the endless list of rules.

Marie attended the royal children in the morning, while the King was closeted with his advisors, dealing with the affairs of state that he hated so much, and the Queen in her private apartments issued instructions to the crowds of dressmakers, shoemakers and milliners who waited upon her.

The Queen's closest companions among the senior ladies of the court were the Princesse de Lamballe and Gabrielle, the lively, pretty Duchesse de Polignac. The golden-haired Princesse, whom the Queen called by her first name, Thérèse, was known to be the most delicate and most sensitive lady at court: she was famous for fainting without warning. Once she passed out when she caught sight of a large red lobster in a painting. On another occasion, when the Queen was giving birth to her first child, a girl, and the whole court had assembled in her bedchamber to watch, the Princesse, overcome with emotion, the heat and the suffocating presence of so many burly men, lost consciousness for several hours.

Gabrielle de Polignac was a much more robust character. Nevertheless the future held pains and trials which would bring both women hard down to earth. Indeed Marie could not have imagined that Gabrielle de Polignac would one day die of despair and disappointment, driven out of France and far away, nor the terrible circumstances in which she would look into the Princesse de Lamballe's piercing blue eyes for the last time.

Marie could sense that the King, beneath his awkward manner, was a kindly man, but he was hardly, she thought secretly, *kingly*. In private, and sometimes in public, he was fond of practical jokes and horseplay. He would try and trip up his pages with his ornamental sash, would pull faces and run away when his valet handed him his nightgown, and sometimes he wandered out of his private chambers into the palace corridors with his breeches hanging round his ankles.

In fact, King Louis didn't really look like a monarch at all; barely five foot six, he was plump and clumsy, with blubbery lips and a drooping white chin that bubbled out of his fat white neck. When taking part in state processions, he appeared, as the Comtesse de la Tour du Pin observed, 'like a peasant shambling along behind his plough'. The court would politely look away when he tripped over his ceremonial sword and went sprawling, or when he mistook one of his wife's ladies in waiting for the Russian ambassador (he was acutely short-sighted, but no King could be permitted to be seen wearing the pince-nez spectacles of a lowly clerk or a schoolteacher). At even the grandest public occasions it was Louis' habit to fall asleep as soon as he was comfortably seated.

At noon the entire royal family would meet in the candlelit, incense-scented chapel for the Catholic ceremony of Mass. They would then take their lunch together in public, surrounded by members of the enormous household all seated on stools of descending height and watched from a distance by humbler servants and invited guests. Marie-Antoinette would eat heartily, while the ladies in waiting pecked nervously at their food, but the King was always in his element. Ignoring the lords in waiting who seemed never to know whether to eat from their own plates or to guide dishes towards the King with little shoves and flutterings of their hands, he tugged the dishes to him and deftly picked at the choicest pieces with surprisingly delicate fingers. Sometimes he would place a morsel in his wife's mouth, although by tradition they never exchanged a word.

On one occasion Marie, tired of the rich food and ignored by the fawning courtiers, kept a beady eye on the king and made a mental note of what he ate: four cutlets, a chicken, half a pheasant, a plateful of ham, half a dozen eggs in sauce and two bottles of champagne. Then he started on the sorbets and sweet-meats.

CHAPTER THREE

Marie became fond of her royal pupils, whom she taught on three mornings each week. On the other two days she was free to wander the grounds and fill her sketchbooks with studies of architecture and wildlife.

The eldest child, nine year-old Marie-Thérèse, was a cheerful girl and in time became an excellent student. Sometimes her shy, serious little brother, the *Dauphin* (the prince and heir) would be allowed to leave his reading and writing lessons and join her for an hour or so. Sometimes, too, the Princesse de Lamballe or the children's governess, Madame de Tourzel, would find time to sit alongside and dab delicately at their easels, until they were called away or lost interest. In the after-noons Marie gave private lessons to Madame Elisabeth, the King's sister, in a little drawing room where a lady in waiting would sharpen Elisabeth's pencils and clean and pass her her brushes, curtseying each time she did so. Madame Elisabeth had no talent for drawing at all, but she was gracious and patient. She was four years younger than Marie but looked five years older. 'She seems so serious,' Marie thought to herself, 'and so anxious that her beauty has already quite faded away.'

Madame Elisabeth was the most religious member of the family. She prayed constantly, and when she left her house in the Versailles grounds she would stop every few paces to kiss one of the crucifixes that her ladies in waiting carried at all times. Marie's most important job was to teach Elisabeth to make waxwork statuettes of saints. When they had finished working, Elisabeth and Marie played cards or went together to distribute money to the poor. Soon Marie Grosholtz was invited to move into Madame Elisabeth's quarters to keep her company in the daytime and to sleep in the adjoining chamber so that her mistress did not feel lonely at night.

King Louis sometimes called unannounced on his younger sister. Often he asked to borrow money from her to pay his debts. But Elisabeth was firm: 'My money, sir, is to be used for the church and for the poor and not for your extravagance!' As his majesty stamped past in a quivering fury, Marie would try to hide herself behind the door of the antechamber.

Once or twice a week Marie was invited to join the whole family in the evening, when a play might be performed for their majesties in the *Salle de Spectacle*, a hall as big as three full-size theatres. As she looked down from the balustraded box at the little figures strutting on the stage below, illuminated by giant candelabras and enormous chandeliers, or when she took part in the great outdoor picnics on the lawns, she felt as if she and all the others present were characters in some wonderful but incomprehensible romantic story, or players in an endless, complicated game.

Sometimes the royal children themselves seemed to her like marionettes in a puppet show, or characters from a pack of playing cards. These thoughts came back to Marie when she was eventually allowed to begin her great work, the turning of the whole family into models, to form a life-size tableau for exhibition in Curtius' wax museum.

It was Marie's own idea to portray the family seated round a small table as if they had gathered for an intimate dinner: this would allow her to place her figures close together, to show them to the world not just as royalty but as loving parents and adoring children.

She had to work quickly; a royal family could not be expected to sit and pose for long, and the suggestion of placing the moulds over their faces was angrily refused (old Monsieur Voltaire had not objected, only joked that at his age every mask was likely to be his death-mask), so likenesses had to be taken with knife and clay and measurements with lengths of string. Luckily Madame de Tourzel persuaded the

Queen to donate a set of the family's third-best clothing and one of the King's old wigs to dress the models in. Marie Antoinette also gave locks of her own hair, to be supplemented by clippings from the servants and the tails of thoroughbred horses from the royal stables.

This was the most ambitious project Marie had ever attempted, but she was quite sure of her skills. Curtius' diligent apprentice had turned into an artist and perfectionist. And she would work day and night, if necessary, to get her models right.

The clay portraits became the moulds over which molten wax was poured. Once the wax had cooled and hardened into a ghostly sheen, Marie would paint on the blush of the cheeks and the red of the lips with expert brushstrokes. The bodies were simple frames of wood with wires bent around them to suggest natural curves under the carefully fastened clothing. When each figure was half-finished it was packed into a closed cart, looking still like a scarecrow or a corpse from the gallows, and taken into Paris to the studio. There, under Marie's stern supervision, a button-maker inserted the eyes and seamstresses completed the stockings and ruffs.

When they were taken to inspect the finished works, even the haughtiest of the courtiers were silenced by the masterpiece that confronted them. They gazed wide-eyed at the breathtakingly realistic faces, at the bodies so exact in size and weight. This was no sculpture in cold, colourless marble or stone; it was like a painting come to life. No – it was even more uncannily real, a set of breathing human beings, made of flesh and blood but frozen in an instant for all time.

CHAPTER FOUR

The court at Versailles seemed like a world apart; sometimes Marie could not believe that that vast enchanted estate with its terraces, paths, fountains and palaces of endless echoing corridors, like a fairyland surrounded by forest, was part of the same world as the city of Paris. Yet the teeming capital was only twelve miles away. Loud and full of bustle, it smelled of perfumes, spices and cooked meats, and other terrible, evil smells from the gutters, the dunghills along the River Seine and the open spaces where executions – hangings and beheadings – were carried out in public. The air was full of rumours, too – plots and gossip, much of it directed at the Queen. More and more people were talking of an end to tyranny, of overturning the old order, throwing out the aristocrats and the traitors once and for all.

Marie marvelled at the ordinary Parisians' love of pleasure and swaggering display, so different from the sombre Swiss among whom she had grown up. But she was frightened by the speed with which their merry-making could turn to violent anger, and a dancing crowd become a howling, threatening mob. She was shocked above all by the scandalous pamphlets that were circulating freely all over the city now, stirring up the people to the bloodiest revenge on their 'enemies' – the aristocrats and the foreigners. She never allowed herself to look at these pamphlets and posters with their grotesque and shocking illustrations, but the contents were unavoidable, declaimed aloud on every street corner for those citizens who could not read.

Marie would make regular Sunday visits to the city, and recently she had noticed a change in the sort of men she encountered at her uncle's house. The clever doctor had sensed which way the wind was blowing. In public he was seen at royal receptions and aristocratic parties, but in private he had begun to entertain a new breed of celebrity – the political agitators and free-thinkers who he had decided were the men of the future. He and his new friends talked so earnestly and heatedly of rights and liberties that the debates often lasted through the night. Marie felt increasingly uneasy these days as she left the likes of the pock-marked pamphleteer, Jacques Pierre, and the renegade priest, Sieyès, behind her in Paris, and emerged from the carriage at Versailles to meet their sworn enemies, among them the King's brothers, the Comte d'Artois and the Comte de Provence. The battle-lines were being drawn.

Provence, known simply as 'Monsieur', was an extravagant and sickly fop, a snob who refused even to *speak* to his social inferiors, which meant he remained haughtily silent for much of the day. Strangely, Monsieur developed a passion for the serious young tutor and teased Marie and flirted with her whenever they met. One day as they passed on a staircase in the palace, Provence lunged forward and tried to embrace her. Without thinking, Marie slapped him full in the face. She fled to her room and locked the doors, terrified of what might happen to her. 'What if his lordship tells the King that I led him on – or even that it was I who threw myself upon him?' That evening Madame Elisabeth took her aside. 'Do not fear,' she said, 'My brother has confessed to me and I have told him off for his ungentlemanly behaviour. Nothing more will be said of it.'

The youngest brother, Artois, was a dashing sportsman and a reckless gambler whose debts would have bankrupted a smaller kingdom. Like Monsieur he was convinced that kings were appointed by God to rule and he loudly threatened several times a day to 'draw the sword of my fathers to defend the honour of my family'. The most sinister member of that family was the Duc D'Orléans, a deceptively charming, dapper figure, who always lagged behind in royal processions as if he did not want to be associated with his cousin the King, and the Queen. Out on the streets Louis and

Marie-Antoinette would be greeted by a few half-hearted cheers, but Orléans, a close friend of many innkeepers and an even more intimate companion of actresses, dancers and serving girls, would be heartily applauded when he passed by.

Marie realised uncomfortably that she was living in two opposing worlds. At court there were reminders of her other life at her uncle's house in Paris. She knew well enough that the 'damned Necker' whom the King cursed aloud, and Baron Necker, the Minister of Finance, the man in charge of the country's money, to whom she had shown her drawings in her uncle's chambers, were one and the same. The Baron was now openly trying to make the King change his ways, and see that he could not carry on flaunting his wealth when his people were going hungry. Marie smiled when the Baron snorted at her little watercolours of the gatherings in the palace gardens, and smiled again when the Queen stamped angrily on the polished floor of her drawing room and, in her German accent, condemned 'that common rogue, that so-called Baron', who had refused again to pay her million-*livre* clothing bill.

But she was careful not to smile and kept her mouth tightly shut when the name of Mirabeau was whispered fearfully by the King's coachmen. Marie knew this adventurer and political agitator well from her uncle's dinner table, and in spite of his frightening appearance (he had been born with only two teeth, a bull's head and popping eyes, and then been horribly disfigured by smallpox scars), she admired him for his overwhelming energy. She knew Mirabeau was involved with the others in her uncle's schemes to overthrow the monarchy, but that was his affair; she was more interested in trying to catch a likeness of that massive, fearful head of his for her sketchbook.

***

As for the most talked-about woman in France, the Queen herself, Marie could not say that she knew her well, although she had been in her presence many times. She couldn't match the Marie-Antoinette who sat for her, fidgeting but smiling while her portrait was painted, with the 'faithless wife', 'cruel mother' and 'scheming Austrian-born traitor' described by the pamphlets out on the streets – the monster that Uncle Philippe's new friends denounced with such furious flourishes at his dinner table.

The Queen was, it was true, high-spirited and saucy, impatient with commoners and quite unwilling to try to please her many enemies. To annoy sticklers for etiquette like the Comtesse de Noailles (who, it was said, had not spoken to one of her closest friends for years after this lady had misplaced a pin on her gown), she would throw her hat into a lake if the fancy took her. She also took great delight in applauding loudly at musical evenings (ladies in those days were forbidden to clap and cheering was unthinkable) and openly teasing her husband.

Defying and terrifying the whole court, she bought herself a gig and galloped round the palace grounds at breakneck speed. Once when she had fallen from a donkey, Marie went nervously to offer her her hand, but Marie-Antoinette refused. 'No,' she laughed, 'I shall lie here until the Comtesse de Noailles comes to explain to me the proper way to rise after such a fall!'

On fine days Marie would accompany the Queen, along with the royal governess, Madame de Tourzel, and Madame Gabrielle and the children to the Petit Trianon, a little lodge hidden in a corner of the vast palace grounds. Here the Queen had built a miniature village where she and her closest companions could spend the day pretending to be non-royals. They would dress up in simple muslin dresses with straw hats and baskets and play at being shepherdesses and dairy-maids, petting tethered lambs and calves and decorating them with flowers. Elaborate games were arranged for King Louis, too, as on one cold February day when he was encouraged to go alone and in disguise to a poor peasant cottage and give money to the terrified creatures huddled inside, but Marie was never quite sure whether he knew when he was play-acting and when he was not.

As for their young tutor, Marie knew that she was just as sensitive as the Princesse de Lamballe, and cleverer by far than her royal pupils and their attendants, but she must never show it. Better to be the brisk and bustling girl with the artistic gift: always 'Young Miss Marie', and never the German-sounding 'Grosholtz', which no one but the Queen knew how to pronounce.

CHAPTER FIVE

In those days before cinema or television, when theatre entertainments and even books were too expensive for most people, the waxworks was a place of special magic. Lit by dazzling chandeliers and decorated with rich tapestries, the museum created a fantasy in which fabulous characters from ancient history rubbed shoulders with the famous heroes – and villains – of the present day. When Marie's tableau of the royal family was finally unveiled, it was the talk of Paris. Although it stood in pride of place in the cabinet of Dr Curtius, everybody knew that it had been sculpted by the young Swiss prodigy, Mademoiselle Marie. And everyone wanted to see it – Royalists and

Republicans alike jostled each other to get a closer view of the remarkable structure; the closest, they thought then, that they would ever come to actual royalty. As she did throughout her life, Marie sat at the entrance to the cabinet and collected the coins herself, studying the reactions of her public.

The Royalists' eyes twinkled with adoration as they studied the detail in the expressions of their dear King and Queen. But the Republicans' eyes glittered with hatred and envy: why should this one family be marked out for such supreme power and influence? They had done nothing to deserve their position, after all. They were just ordinary people like the common citizens over whom they ruled. At the end of the day when the crowds had been turned out and the doors locked behind them, Marie would stand and admire her own work, the waxworks of the King and Queen and their children looked, she thought, much more like a real family than ever their models did at court.

She continued to spend most weeks at Versailles, but one day the long years of the dream came suddenly to an end. A message, carried by a groom in disguise, arrived from Curtius. 'Pretend to be ill – swoon and call for a physician; demand to be brought here, to Paris, immediately.'

Marie could not guess what had happened, but she knew she had to act at once and do just as her uncle had said. She hurried as fast as her petticoats would allow down the great sweep of stone steps into the servants' annex, calling out for help as she burst breathless and perspiring into a scullery. To her astonishment the room was already full of washerwomen, cooks and gardeners rushing hither and thither wild-eyed, flustered and dishevelled, all speaking at once. She stood unnoticed at the doorway and listened until at last she made out the words – '...Mirabeau and the representatives of the People have taken power. They have forced the King to swear an oath of loyalty to them! *It is the end of the monarchy*!' Clutching her forehead to feign illness, Marie ordered the servants to bring her a doctor and a carriage at once.

***

For weeks after Mirabeau and his supporters overthrew the government there was chaos in France; many who hated the old system and wanted reform nonetheless still hoped they could keep the monarchy; others were determined to get rid of kings for good. While the two sides raged at each other, Louis remained officially in charge.

Trouble had been brewing in France for years. Under their cruel rulers, the French people had suffered terribly. A man or woman could be thrown into prison without reason if a lord or lady ordered it: landlords could take away their tenants' property without paying them a sou; and on occasions when the poor and starving peacefully protested, the King's supporters simply had their leaders hanged. When people turned to the church for help, its priests told them that God, too, would punish them if they did not do as they were told. And even now, as his subjects became angrier and more desperate, King Louis and the court still refused to change their ways. When his popular minister, Necker, stood up to him yet again and demanded fairer government, Louis dismissed him. Baron Necker and the Duc D'Orléans now both openly declared their support for the Republican side, and fled from Paris before they could be imprisoned. Louis, in an increasing state of panic, ordered foreign soldiers to surround the city to keep order.

On a Sunday afternoon in July an angry armed crowd of six thousand people gathered in the centre of Paris and called on all the citizens of France to join them. Their pleas for better treatment were turning into demands for absolute freedom for all. Marie listened from the window of Curtius's study in the Boulevard du Temple as the roar of the mob came nearer. In a few minutes the crowd was pressing at the gates outside and its leaders were shouting the name of Curtius, insisting that the doctor open the door.

'We want Necker! We want Orléans!' they bellowed. 'Give us the busts from your exhibition, let us have our heroes!' Smiling nervously, Curtius unlocked the iron gates and Marie and the servants carefully delivered the two heads which were seized, stuck on poles and carried away in triumph at the head of the howling, chanting procession.

CHAPTER SIX

The drama at Marie's doorstep was the very first act in an uprising that swept France and became known as the French Revolution. At the Place Vendôme in central Paris, the King's troops charged the crowd, killing several of them. Necker's wax head was cut clean in half by a sabre, but the bust of Orléans was returned to the museum in one piece.

While the King and Queen and their courtiers watched helplessly from Versailles, the country seethed. As for the flamboyant Doctor Curtius, after months of secret preparation he was now able to switch effortlessly from his role as friend of royalty and hob-nobber with the nobility into 'Citizen Curtius', the keenest supporter of the Revolution. Marie Grosholtz, as ever, found herself caught between two worlds: she sympathised with the poor who had risen in revolt against the injustices of the old order, but she could not forget the kindnesses that the royal family had shown her. She kept her thoughts to herself, but the knot of fear inside her told her that even more dreadful things were about to happen.

In a few days the mob had grown into a huge, angry throng. The protestors now went in search of gunpowder for their muskets and cannons. They decided to march to the old prison-fortress of the Bastille, where they knew there were hundreds of barrels of the stuff. They stormed the building, released a handful of poor prisoners who had been kept there in chains for years, then beheaded the governor and another official not even listening to their cries of surrender. This time it was two real heads which were stuck on pikes and carried triumphantly to Dr Curtius. The enterprising showman had agreed to copy them in wax to add to what he was now calling 'the People's Museum'.

'This must be done at once,' ordered her uncle, 'but as you know, I do not have the stomach for it, so you, Marie, must take the moulds of the dead faces. I will then finish the likenesses off myself.'

Marie did not hesitate. She was used to obeying her uncle and she saw in his eyes not only the glint of fear as the mob bayed outside, but the spark of a new opportunity. The waxworks already featured several death-masks, moulds taken from the faces of famous people (for in the 18th century, before there were cameras to preserve our images, even humble families sometimes paid for casts or portraits of their dead relatives). What Marie did not yet know was that the glassy-eyed, open-mouthed faces on the table in front of her were just the first in a long, deathly procession.

After the Bastille had fallen, and the city had become calm again for a moment, Marie and her uncle visited the remains of the fortress and peered into the dark dungeons below the squat towers. Marie was struck by the crowds of sightseers who were also wandering the ruins, and noticed how they were all drawn to the grimmest, most gloomy parts of the building, breathing in the foul smells, pointing out the shadows of the toads, rats and lizards that infested the place, inspecting the iron cages and torture instruments and telling each other gruesome stories of the terrible things that had gone on there. People were thrilled by horror, she thought, much more than by beauty and goodness.

On 5 October 1789 an enormous mob, led by screaming women from the Paris streets and followed by revolutionary soldiers, marched to Versailles and broke into the Queen's private rooms there. Louis, Marie-Antoinette and their children tried to conceal themselves but the invaders smashed down the panels of the secret room where they were hiding. They pushed them roughly into one of the smallest of their ornate carriages and escorted them back to Paris. As the carriage swayed, the horses snorting fearfully, the crowd cursed and spat and danced around their prisoners.

The new revolutionary leaders ordered that Marie's

models of the royal family at dinner be taken from the Paris showroom all the way back to the abandoned gardens at Versailles and put on display where ordinary people could view their hated rulers, surrounded by the luxuries that they had so selfishly enjoyed. The inside of the palace was turned into a freak-show with scare-crows dragged in from the fields and propped up among the wreckage of the ornate furniture in mockery of the palace's former inhabitants. Pigs and goats wandered through the empty chambers.

As for the real royal family, they were shut up inside the Tuileries Palace, where Parisians could come and peer over the walls at them as they walked miserably back and forth in the gardens. Louis seemed to accept his fate in dignified silence, but the Queen knew that their lives were now in real danger. She persuaded the King that their only hope was to flee the country in disguise with the children. One night, with the help of the Queen's devoted admirer, the dashing Count Axel von Fersen, they managed to slip out of the Tuileries into a closed carriage. Inside was Madame de Tourzel pretending to be a baroness; the King and Queen played the parts of her servants and Fersen was the coachman. The big heavy carriage trundled painfully slowly through the night, but the plan was bungled. The loyal soldiers who were supposed to meet them halfway were not there and the family were recognised by angry villagers before they could reach the Austrians waiting at the border. This time they were brought back and imprisoned in the Temple, an even smaller building where their brutal gaolers watched them day and night. Even the most loyal supporters of the monarchy gave up hope: Gabrielle de Polignac, the Comte d'Artois and Comte de Provence and many others escaped from France, which was now officially proclaimed a Republic.

Curtius, however, who had been busily working to keep in favour with the new regime, went from strength to strength. His house was still the Republicans' favourite meeting-place and in gratitude they appointed him commander of their new local police force, the National Guard. He enjoyed his new role, designed fancy uniforms for himself and his troops, and soon began to boast of the heroic deeds he had carried out for the People and for Liberty.

It seemed as if in an instant the old France had disappeared. Everyone in Paris was breathless with excitement – and fear. Everything was possible now, and there was a feeling that anything at all might happen at any moment. The strangest collection of characters banded together in the name of the Revolution. Along with soldiers, priests, writers, adventurers and ruffians were even stranger creatures like the mad Dutch nobleman, Anarchasis Cloots, who dressed in a fantastic homemade costume covered in moons and stars and proclaimed that he had been sent by the Spirit of the Universe to save the world.

Everything had turned upside down. The poor were putting feathers and flowers in their hats and nobles were wrapping themselves in filthy cast-offs so as not to be recognised in the streets. The powdered wigs and silk knee-breeches that fine gentlemen used to wear were suddenly out of fashion: most of the rebel soldiers were dirty, ragged and proudly called themselves *Sans Culottes*, (ie men 'without breeches'). Curtius told Marie to alert the dressmaker and overnight the doorman at the wax museum had swapped his satin brocades for the new uniform of a red Liberty cap and striped cotton trousers.

CHAPTER SEVEN

Some of Marie's relatives from Berne had enlisted in the King's Swiss Guard. This was a regiment of hand-picked troops loyal to the monarchy who swore to defend the French royal family to the death if necessary. They got their chance when an army of citizens, waving pikes and axes and firing captured muskets, overran the pleasure gardens around the Palace of the Tuileries. The brave Swiss soldiers formed ranks and stood their ground, but their French officers deserted them, the cannons they had sent for never came, and within an hour it was all over – the crack-crack of gunfire, the cries of battle and the jangling church bells sounding the alarm across the city died away to silence.

Before the sun rose the following day Marie, alone and disguised as a beggarwoman, picked her way through the bodies still scattered where they had fallen among the toppled statues and shattered urns, searching for a familiar face. At the very end of the battle one or two guardsmen had torn off their bright-coloured uniforms and tried to escape, but they had been hunted down and shot or stabbed where they hid. Not one of Marie's uncles or cousins survived.

Any members of the nobility who had survived the Revolution by hiding out did not last much longer. A few hours after the drastic defeat of the Swiss Guard, Madame de Tourzel, the royal governess, and the Princess de Lamballe took the risk of leaving the house where they had been comfortably confined to take food to some terrified neighbours. The two women were pulled from their coach by a gang of revolutionaries, separated and dragged through the streets in triumph. They were thrown into dank cells where rats scuttled out to nibble at their silk-stockinged toes.

Two weeks later Marie was called from her home by

the revolutionaries, told to bring plaster, a water-bottle and a knife, and hustled through the onlookers to a filthy alley behind the prison of 'La Force'. Suddenly a toothless, bare-chested Sans Culotte turned to her, grinning, and pulled something from the butcher's bucket he was carrying. Despite the smears of blood, Marie recognised the golden curls and pink cheeks of the Princesse de Lamballe. She was commanded there and then to take a cast of the severed head of her old friend, to turn into another trophy for exhibition in the People's Museum. Surrounded by a rapt audience, Marie, silent and expressionless, did as she was ordered.

CHAPTER EIGHT

For two whole years there was chaos while the Republican leaders tried to decide how to run the nation and fight off their many enemies. As the politicians argued, mobs of ordinary people, drunk with their new power, roamed Paris taking revenge on anyone they thought might be a Royalist. In the frenzy even women and children were not safe; the young were cut down along with the old and soon guilt or innocence did not count at all. The authorities did nothing to stop the killing; they only helped to speed up the endless official executions by setting up their own terrible death machine. It was a kindly doctor, Monsieur Guillotin, who had invented the contraption, hoping to lessen the suffering of condemned prisoners by giving them a quick, clean death. He had never imagined that his 'guillotine' would one day be used to terrorise the entire nation.

Even in the middle of the madness, Marie's expert eye picked out all the details of the faces, the expressions and gestures and the clothing that people wore and filed them away in her memory. She met the revolutionary ringleaders and came to know their wives, their companions and the hangers-on who clustered round them. She saw how power changed them all sooner or later, from eager freedom-fighters into cruel, thoughtless tyrants.

The men she had seen plotting round her uncle's table were all now famous names: Mirabeau had died of exhaustion, but Robespierre, Marat and Danton were very much alive.

'Robespierre pretended to be a Sans Culotte,' Marie said later, 'but his blue silk frock-coats and lace collars were always chosen with taste and his hair was constantly powdered and rearranged.' He wore little green spectacles on the end of his snub nose.

The toad-like Marat suffered from a hideous skin disease which also made his body smell revolting. From the very beginning he had threatened his enemies with horrific vengeance. 'Three hundred aristocrats' heads must be struck off before Liberty is established!' he had told Marie, months before the killings actually started. Later he changed his mind: 'I have calculated that we can, if we work hard, kill 26,000 of them in a single day!'

When the massacres were being carried out, or when one or another group got the upper hand, Marat would disappear into one of the secret underground hideouts he had prepared around the city. He would then wait until he was sure that his friends were still in control before coming up into the light to find another crowd to roar his threats at. Respectable citizens were terrified of Marat, but the mob loved him; he dressed in the simple clothes they wore and rarely washed, and his official lodgings were poor and bare. Despite his appearance, though, he was no common thug, but an educated man who had travelled widely, even qualifying as a doctor in Scotland.

For some of the time during 1791 and 1792 the giant Danton was in command, and to begin with Marie thought that he was nobler than the rest. Danton, whose brilliant speeches could win over anyone who listened, took a liking to Marie and invited her to all the celebrations that the new government was organising.

The common people of Paris still admired their new leaders even if they could not understand their constant feuding and the sudden falls from favour. Most Parisians had only heard from others of the revolutionaries' exploits; they were eager to see what their champions really looked like and Curtius lost no time in obliging them. The wax exhibition filled up with the heads of the living – Danton, Marat, Robespierre and the others – all looking across from their pedestals to the other end of the room where the faces of their victims stared back. Marie had never been busier.

***

In January 1793 Marat and Robespierre finally persuaded the Assembly which now ruled France to condemn the King to death. Louis' cousin Orléans, who since fleeing Paris with Baron Necker had changed his name to Philippe Egalité ('Equality'), was one of those who signed the death warrant. In April the plump, shortsighted King walked stiffly but proudly up the steps to the guillotine. So many were being executed every day that heads were no longer brought to Marie. When someone special had been guillotined the executioner would tip her off, and she would hurry to the overflowing cemetery at dusk after the carts had all made their deliveries and gone.

On the night of King Louis' execution she rushed to the cemetery with more urgency than usual. As always, a few coins persuaded one of the attendants to find the right victim (his head was lying unnoticed with all the others) and Marie set to work with her clay. Her eyes hardly focused as her busy hands moved. It seemed unbelievable to her that this was the King's face she was touching. And yet it was the ghosts of the living that haunted her more – Marie-Antoinette's face, and the faces of her children, seemed to hover like shadows in the cold darkness in front of her.

In the countryside some citizens began to fight back against the revolutionaries' cruelties. One outraged young lady, the beautiful grey-eyed Charlotte Corday, travelled to Paris and managed to trick her way into Marat's apartment where she stabbed him to death as he lay in his bath.

Marie was called to draw the scene and then went to the prison death-cell where Mademoiselle Corday was sitting patiently awaiting her own end. Marie quickly sketched a likeness and later that evening went to recover the girl's head to take a mould. The waxwork she made of Marat in his bath was put on official display in the centre of Paris. But, among the first small signs that the tide was turning for the revolutionaries, more and more people went quietly to the Palais Royal to look pityingly at poor Charlotte.

On a chilly October morning Marie, wrapped in a shawl, leaned from the open window on the first floor of her uncle's house. Below her in the Boulevard, Queen Marie-Antoinette, looking pale and half-starved, her hair cropped short, sat upright in the cart as it trundled past on its way to the place of execution. The painter Jacques-Louis David, one of the leading revolutionaries, had ordered Marie to make a sketch of the Queen as she passed, but when the moment came Marie found that for once could not control her feelings. She fainted and the sketching-paper fluttered down on to the path below. Still, she was waiting at the cemetery at nightfall and two days later the King and Queen were reunited in the wax museum.

**

There was no one Marie could talk to about what she had seen and what she felt. With her aunt and mother she talked only about cooking and dressmaking and organising the servants; the two old ladies were much too frightened to think about what was really going on outside. Instead, in the moments between huddling under the bedclothes and falling asleep, Marie held solitary conversations in which she asked herself the questions, and replied as best she could.

'Your royal employers are dead, Marie. The little *Dauphin* has disappeared... how is it that you are here, alive, well-fed and praised by everyone as a friend of the Revolution?'

'But you know I could not have saved them; I didn't betray them. I'm only a poor helpless model-maker after all.'

'Who do you take yourself for, young lady? You have held the heads of princesses and queens in your hands; perhaps like the revolutionaries you're secretly ambitious for the power that they once wielded?'

'A strange sort of power! My only subjects are lifeless models; I'm the Queen of the Waxworks, nothing more, an unseen, unknown power behind the scenes... and that's how it must always be.'

The Terror was in full swing, and France's new rulers split into ever smaller squabbling groups, each one trying to get the upper hand by declaring the others traitors to the Revolution. One group after another fell from favour and paid the price. In November the revolutionary council turned on Orléans, the 'friend of the People' and betrayer of his own family. Nobody spoke up in his defence.

Meanwhile, all through the months of the Terror poor Madame Elisabeth, forgotten by everyone in the excitement, had been praying alone in her cell in the Temple. By springtime she was the only one of the royal family left in France, and now she too was paraded, still praying, past the crowds on her way to death. Marie stayed at home that day, closed the shutters and thanked God that no one called her to the cemetery.

It seemed there were almost no aristocrats left to kill, but again and again the members of the National Assembly quarrelled, accused each other of treason and sentenced each other to death. The guillotine took them one by one. Robespierre turned on Danton, then the Assembly turned on Robespierre. The last of the original revolutionaries, those who had been loudest and cruellest in condemning their former friends, were now being condemned themselves. The pitiless judge, Fouquier-Tinville, was quickly sentenced and the monster Hébert, who had whipped up hatred of the Queen with his writing, was dragged off, screaming for the mercy he had never shown to others. Even crazy Anarchasis Cloots was led away in his multicoloured robes, arguing with his fellow-prisoners to the end.

CHAPTER NINE

In the spring of 1794 there were a few weeks of calm, and the new government ordered more festivals to keep the people happy. Curtius was away in the east somewhere on some mysterious 'official business', and Marie tried hard to pretend that life was returning to normal. But just as the noises of the Terror all around her died away, they seemed to grow louder again. The sudden rush of footsteps, the clatter of carts, angry shouting and despairing screams came and went in the distance, through days and then nights, and then she heard them closer to home, in the streets around the big townhouse. Instead of the crack of festive fireworks and the sounds of street musicians, there were gunshots and muffled, menacing drumming.

One night when all the household was asleep there was a thunderous knocking on the big iron gates. Marie, her mother and her aunt, dressed only in night-gowns, half-dreaming and terrified, were grabbed, bundled into an open carriage and driven to the former convent which had become the notorious prison 'La Force'.

There, they were thrust into a cramped cell where twenty other women were already crouching in the darkness on the stinking straw-covered floor. Someone had given their names to the authorities, claiming that they were friends of the royal family, and Marie was sure she knew who that someone was. She had noticed Dutroy, a rogue who danced and pulled faces at a poor little theatre in their neighbourhood, jealously eyeing their rich clothes and the long lines of customers at their museum door. Marie knew that Dutroy was also a sort of informer, paid by Sanson the public execu-tioner to run errands for him, and to supply him with the names of suspected traitors.

It was in this old convent, a grim and terrifying place, that the Princesse de Lamballe had spent her last hours. Each time the heavy doors were unbolted a great shudder ran through the women inside. Their hair had already been hacked short to prepare them for the guillotine, and they expected to be dragged off to their deaths at any moment. Only one among them seemed completely unafraid. The beautiful Josephine de Beauharnais had pleaded in vain to save the life of her own husband, an elderly general who was executed for ordering his army to retreat. While she waited with her two small daughters to find out if she was going to live or die, she tried to cheer up the other women. 'You must never, never give up hope. Remember you are all wives, mothers, daughters. Think of your families and don't despair!'

The lively young widow and the grave little wax-worker instantly became friends, but then Marie was moved to another part of the prison. All she could think about was the hunger, the ache of fear in her stomach, the smell and the damp cold. And then, without any warning, she was suddenly set free. Curtius had asked his commander, General Kléber, and that good revolutionary, the painter David, for help. Grateful to Curtius for his spying (for that was what he had been up to in Germany), and to Marie for her gruesome modelling, the revolutionaries were happy to oblige.

Many of the innocent suspects held that summer were taken to be guillotined, others were murdered in their cells, but a month after Marie was freed Josephine, too, was allowed to return to her family. Marie did not know then that she would meet Josephine again – and not in the midst of a tragedy, but as part of a romantic adventure that would change the whole history of Europe.

***

Late in the hot summer of 1794 Philippe Curtius became gravely ill at his new country house where he had gone to escape from the pressures of Paris. The most expensive physicians could not agree on what was wrong with him – his servants even hinted that he had been poisoned by his enemies.

'It could be the Royalists who have done this!'

'Or the Swiss, or the Germans?'

'Ah, but perhaps it was the revolutionaries themselves?'

'You gossip like empty-headed geese!' scolded Marie, hiding her worry as she paid the doctors' huge fees.

After a month Curtius was getting no better: he had no strength to hold a pen and so he dictated his last will and testament to a clerk, leaving everything he owned in the world to Marie. By early September he could no longer speak. And at the end of the month he died. As it turned out, Marie had been left enormous debts by her extravagant uncle, as well as his houses and exhibitions, so for the next few years she worked even harder, handing over the entrance fees from the waxworks to the bankers, lawyers and landlords, and keeping only a little for herself and her mother.

Gradually the situation in the country began to calm down. The time that people called the Terror gave way to an uneasy peace in Paris. But France was still at war with its neighbours. And, though its strong revolutionary army managed to defend the country, at home a weak government struggled to keep control as prices rose and people went hungry again. What little money people had rapidly lost its value and Marie, like everyone else, had to grow vegetables in her garden and keep chickens to survive. The money collected from the shows was now just a worthless trickle.

'The boasters and the bullies are still in power,' she told her old mother 'but there are no strong men any more.'

In fact, there was one – an unknown Corporal from the island of Corsica named Napoleon Bonaparte whom the people were soon hailing as a new national hero. When he stepped forward to take command and save the nation, Bonaparte took the old Roman title of Consul instead of King, and claimed for himself not only France but also Marie's old friend Josephine de Beauharnais.

Romantics everywhere were charmed by the story of their love. However, the new Consul, who had come straight from the army, had other passions which were more cause for alarm: his favourite pastime was setting off the biggest barrages of cannon-fire that anyone had ever seen.

CHAPTER TEN

On a chilly grey morning in 1800, a flunkey ushered Marie into the warm room and helped her with the bags of plaster, the bottles of oil and cloths that she had brought. There, alone in the middle of the floor sat Napoleon, a small fierce-looking man on an ornate chair posing with his chin resting on his hand. Only his lips moved from time to time as officers approached to bow and murmur in his ear. On a couch behind him Josephine, still beautiful, draped in skimpy lace, was laughing with another finely dressed woman. When they saw Marie the two women rose, smiling, to welcome her; but the little figure sat unmoving, gazing sternly into space.

With all her knowledge of good manners, Marie was not sure how to address the man who had just overthrown the French government and was hoping to conquer all of Europe.

'If you please Your Excellency,' she tried, 'I must first oil your face before applying the wet plaster...' As she began to smear the gobbets of plaster across his smooth and chubby features, Marie readied the two goose-quills that she would place in his nostrils so that he could breathe under the mask. This was always the most uncomfortable part for her models, so she was ever careful to reassure them.

'Do not be alarmed...' she said to Napoleon, at which he almost leapt from the chair.

'Madame, *I* would not be alarmed even if you surrounded my head with loaded pistols!'

'I-I humbly beg your pardon, Sir,' she stuttered, but Josephine clasped her hand, and with the other stroked her husband's shoulder soothingly.

As he settled back into his chair, Josephine took Marie aside: 'Please do be careful and treat our Consul gently – it was very difficult for me to persuade him to sit for you.' Marie went back to work, moulding quickly and skilfully, then wiped the plaster and oil away. Bonaparte's expression never changed. As soon as most of the plaster was gone he began again to bark commands to the messengers who darted in and out. His only other words to Marie were a brisk '*Merci Madame, et au revoir,*' as she gathered up her things and bowed before leaving.

Later, after sending him his sculpted head, Marie heard that the great Bonaparte was delighted with the likeness. He soon sent his generals Masséna and Moreau and his Chancellor Cambacérès to be modelled, too.

Four years later the little Consul declared himself Emperor and set off with his soldiers to win an Empire. Napoleon's armies rolled across Europe, defeating Austria and occupying Italy and Spain, then crossing into Egypt on the way to challenge the British in India. It looked as if only the English heroes Wellington and Nelson stood between Bonaparte and his dream of conquering the world. He was certainly the most famous man of the day, loved by the French (in Paris the ancient roman fashions he favoured were all the rage), admired by many Europeans but hated and feared by others as a ruthless dictator. In Britain the little Emperor, who was nicknamed 'Boney', became a legendary bogeyman, used to frighten naughty children in puppet-shows and bedtime stories.

***

Marie was now in her late thirties. Most women of her age had been married for years and were raising large families, but since her mother and aunt had died she had lived alone except for the servants. She had learned not to trust in fate, and not to rely upon other people, especially not the glamorous and powerful. Her work had kept her occupied and made her prosperous and perhaps it had also protected her from danger – indeed her work was still the most important thing in her life. But, for an ambitious man, what a catch this wealthy spinster would make!

François Tussaud, who had been in charge of uncle Philippe's travelling shows and now worked for Marie as a manager, had lately begun to talk to her in a different way, more like a close friend than an employee. 'You need a man to be a husband and a business partner,' he kept on telling her, 'And most of all to be a father to your children before you are too old.'

'He is too forward,' she thought, 'but perhaps he is right.' He was likeable enough, and – thank God – neither glamorous nor powerful, the type of man who could provide a quiet, settled life and perhaps some heirs who could carry on the family business. Still, François had to propose several times before the independent Marie felt ready to accept.

CHAPTER ELEVEN

Madame Marie Tussaud soon had two young sons, but somehow she seemed to be working as hard as ever to pay all the bills and to keep the museum and the travelling exhibitions going. Much to her regret, François had turned out to be idle and extravagant: he spent much more than he earned, and the business ventures he persuaded her to put her money into never seemed to succeed.

When, in 1802, a peace treaty was signed at last between France and her old enemy Britain, Marie decided to take her waxworks exhibition across the Channel and try her luck in that rich new market. Taking her elder boy Joseph, whom she nicknamed

'Nini', and a servant with her, she arrived in London and set up first at the Lyceum Theatre in the Strand. England at that time had plenty of attractions – Major Astley's circus and funfairs and sideshows – but nothing like this, an entertainment put together by someone who had actually lived through the French Revolution, someone who had actually met the King of France and poor Queen Marie-Antoinette. The show was a sensation. To build a name for herself, Marie resolved to take her collection of sixty figures, pictures and mementos on tour, as she had done in France .

While she was travelling around the country, Marie learned that her old friend Napoleon was being held under guard not so very far away on Britain's south coast. After years of warfare on land and sea and winning and then losing his empire, in 1815 Napoleon had been captured by the British, who decided not to execute him but to send him into exile 3,000 miles away on their tiny island of St Helena. Marie had followed the Emperor's exploits in the newspapers. She found his story with its breathtaking victories, horrific defeats and sudden changes of fortune more exciting than any novel. Never believing it would be allowed, she now asked if she could see the most famous prisoner of all, to model him again. While he waited for the fleet to escort him, the ex-Emperor was being held aboard the warship *Bellerophon* anchored off the coast of Devon, where dozens of tiny boats crowded the Channel as journalists, local dignitaries and sightseers struggled for a glimpse of him.

In the end, Marie decided not to wait for permission. She left her assistants to watch over the exhibition and hired a coach to take her at full speed to the town of Torquay. By a stroke of luck His Worship the Mayor had visited her waxworks once in London, and the naval officers knew of her by reputation. A boat and crew were immediately put at Madame's disposal.

Just as when she had first seen him fifteen years before, Napoleon was speechless, but this time, Marie thought, it was with astonishment and confusion at seeing her again. The little man was thinner in the face, his hair just a few grey wisps, but he still sat stiff and proud. This time Marie had no time to apply her oil and plaster, but was allowed just ten minutes to sit and sketch while the English officers watched. Bonaparte threw back his head, then froze in that imperial pose. Marie thought she caught the faintest hint of a smile.

'Have I changed so much?' he asked her in French.

'Very little, sir,' she replied.

'Ah, but my fortunes are much changed since we last met.'

'Indeed, sir, and in a small way so are mine.'

In the event, Napoleon escaped from the British, and was defeated and exiled again. This time he did not survive for long. Even after his death Bonaparte was good to Marie. For sixpence the visitors to her travelling show could examine various mementos of his life that Marie collected from all over Europe: his carriage, his bed, his comb, watch, toothbrush, stockings, underpants and even one of his teeth which had been removed, slowly and painfully, by the St Helena surgeon as the little man silently fumed.

Meanwhile, in Italy the French Royalists in exile declared that the Comte de Provence (the man who had pounced on Marie on the stairs at Versailles) was now King, and, when Napoleon was finally defeated, Provence returned to restore the monarchy in France. It amused Marie to think that she had slapped the face of the man who was now King Louis XVIII.

When this Louis died, his younger brother, the Comte d'Artois, whom Marie had known as a wild young spendthrift, succeeded him as King Charles X. However, still a figure of fun, he was chased from the throne after only a few weeks. From the safety of England, Marie watched the political squabbles, the uncertainties of life in France, and decided, once and for all, not to go back to her former home.

CHAPTER TWELVE

T he more money I make in England, and in
Scotland and Ireland,' Marie complained, 'the
more François seems to be losing in Paris.' Marie had
left her second son, François junior, with his father in
Paris. Now, after two years of constant travelling, she
sent for the boy to come and live with her. 'From now
on,' she thought to herself, 'François Tussaud senior
can manage on his own.'

Marie became used to England, to loading and
unloading her trunks from the stagecoach, to negotiating with landladies and theatre managers, hiring local
servants and outwitting the swindlers and thieves and
crooked lawyers who preyed on the handful of women

who dared to do business on their own in those days. She enjoyed being in charge, keeping the others in order, greeting the admiring customers, counting the takings. She even enjoyed the rush to create new models to keep her hungry public happy. Other entertainers tried to copy her, but they could never equal her modelling skills – or match the enormous sums she spent on costumes and scenery. 'I have done what Napoleon never did,' she joked to young Joseph, 'I have conquered all of England without firing a shot!'

Glasgow, Newcastle, York, Leeds, Taunton, Portsmouth, Canterbury: in the years that followed, Marie and her family criss-crossed the British Isles, stopping and setting up for three weeks here, two months there. She taught Nini and little François to sketch and to model in clay and was pleased to see how quickly they picked up the skills.

By 1820 Madame Tussaud had become a household name, and for weeks before she arrived in a town the newspapers would carry articles promising 'the Greatest, the Grandest Exhibition ever seen in these parts'. In time, the young English Princess Victoria and the Prime Minister were added to the waxwork collection alongside the Tsar of Russia, but it was the famous criminals who drew the biggest crowds. The celebrated Edinburgh grave-robbers Burke and Hare were included, and Marie herself took the mould from the face of 'Stewart the Poisoner', who had murdered a sea-captain and was suspected of murdering nine others.

***

But all was not well in England. By 1830 the citizens here, too, seemed ready to start a revolution against their rich and aristocratic rulers. Thousands and thousands of poor country folk had been forced from their land by ruthless landlords or had to move to the miserable, overcrowded cities to look for work. In the summer of 1831 the people of Birmingham refused to pay their taxes, in Nottingham rioters burned down the castle and there were angry meetings across the West Country.

In the city of Bristol on October 29th of that year, on the same day as the hated Judge Wetherall came from London to try a handful of protestors who had recently been arrested, posters and handbills advertised the arrival of Madame Tussaud with her travelling exhibition. The mood on the crowded streets was ugly and the authorities were afraid that there would be a full-scale uprising. They quickly found a few dozen thugs and bullies and took them on as special constables to help them keep the peace.

As the Judge sat down to dinner in the Mansion House, a mob gathered outside and began to tear the slates from the roof. Cobblestones came flying through the stained-glass windows and the diners rushed for cover. The great doors of the Mansion House were too strong to break down, but some of the attackers managed to smash their way into the cellars where they were confronted with hundreds upon hundreds of bottles of fine wine. For a while the only noises to be heard were gulping and gurgling, then a cry echoed from the cellars – 'If we can't hang the judge, we'll free all the prisoners and burn the town!' The rioters then fell back on to the street, red-faced, dribbling and more murderous than before.

Marie was watching at the door of her lodgings in the elegant Queen's Square when the mob passed by. 'You rich folk get out while you can!' she heard, 'As soon as we get fuel and firewood we'll be back to burn you out!'

Across the city, buildings were being ransacked and set on fire. Marie threw on a shawl and trotted in her little ankle-boots the quarter mile to the Assembly Rooms where workmen were supposed to be setting up the exhibition. The place was quite deserted but, sure enough, there on the door was a big chalk cross – the mark used by the rioters to show which buildings were to be destroyed.

Marie was nearly seventy years old, but she didn't pause for a moment. She hurried back to Queen's Square and called for Nini and François, as well as her maid and the servants to come and help her. The naked wax figures were loaded on to trolleys, trundled out of the Assembly Rooms and piled up together on the pavement. 'Like corpses on the streets of Paris during the Terror,' thought Marie, but she said nothing. She stationed her black doorman, Angelo, to watch over the waxworks and he stood, glaring, dressed in his uniform of a yellow frock-coat and pink pantaloons, with an enormous blunderbuss clutched in his huge fingers. The family lined up behind her, and for three hours the stout little woman with the long nose and owl-glasses kept guard over her priceless belongings and dared anyone to come any closer. Every few minutes wild-eyed looters appeared from out of the smoke, glanced in amazement at the strange little group and disappeared back into the night. By dawn it was safe enough to make their way back across the smouldering square to their lodgings and bolt the door behind them.

The riots went on for three days and nights; all through the fourth day the shouting, explosions and cries of terror could be heard, until, finally, in the evening there was a different noise. To the sound of fifes and the rattling of drums, the army marched into the city. Bristol fell silent, the troublemakers melted away, and Madame Tussaud, her servants and her baggage moved on.

'Were you truly afraid, Madame?' asked her maid when they were safely in the carriage.

'My dear,' Marie replied, 'Perhaps we were in danger, but compared to the Paris mob, this Bristol rabble was a mere street-party.'

CHAPTER THIRTEEN

'Liverpool, Nottingham, Newark, Oxford, Reading, Brighton: for the first time Marie began to feel her age. She was fed up with the uncomfortable stage-coaches and the muddy English highways; as for the new-fangled steam trains, they were too slow and smelled of coal-dust and oil. Those strong fingers that had sculpted so skilfully now shook when she went to sign the bills. For years she had been squirreling away the money that was left over when the bills had all been paid, but now she would have to borrow more if she wanted to settle down at long last. She looked around for a suitable place and found it at the junction of Baker Street and Portman Square in the middle of

London: a magnificent building in which there was the biggest ballroom in Europe – bigger even than the *Salle de Spectacle* at Versailles – and uncle Philippe's museum would have fitted in there twenty times over.

In 1835 there was nobody in England who hadn't heard that Madame Tussaud's illustrious waxworks had now found a permanent home. Marie visited her waxworks every day of the week, always in the same full-length black dress with the same black bonnet on her head.

In Victorian England women were wearing puff sleeves, bright ribbons and huge, hooped skirts, their hair scraped primly into buns after the style of the Queen. But Marie preferred her own style: under her bonnet she wore a bright bandana in the French manner, tying back the ringlets that had now turned to wispy white curls.

'She looks like an old lady from another age,' whispered an attendant, as he listened to Marie telling stories to a group of visitors.

Madame Tussaud loved to describe the characters

she had known, remembering every detail of how they looked, how they spoke. She was fond of handing out advice to the audience that gathered wherever she paused, but she never ever spoke about her own feelings and kept her opinions of all those tyrants, rogues and heroes to herself.

Then, one day, a message arrived from Paris. Marie had not seen her husband since she left for England in 1802, and hadn't had a letter from him for nearly forty years. She knew it could hardly be good news. Monsieur Tussaud was short of money. 'I demand that, as my wife, you send me immediately a half-share of the fortune you have amassed in England!'

When she had left France, Marie had left her husband in charge of all her Parisian businesses and properties, never asking him to send on the money that they brought in, but François was a lazy, feckless good-for-nothing – the money had soon run out, the properties had been sold or lost and the businesses dwindled away. Marie decided to ignore the letter.

But then in 1844 he wrote again. 'I require a large

amount of money to invest in a theatre here in Paris. If you do not send it at once, I shall come to London to claim my part of your businesses there.' Marie shuddered and said nothing. Nini and François junior, who now preferred the English name Francis, wrote back refusing on her behalf.

Nowadays Marie said her prayers more often, although her sons – now middle-aged men with families of their own – noticed that she still used the large black crucifix in her bedchamber as a hatstand. She lectured her children and grandchildren regularly, 'Always beware,' she used to say, 'of the Three Black Crows who will bring you nothing but bad luck: the Doctor, the Lawyer and the Priest.' She still had a sharp tongue. To her manager she said, 'Beware, sir, of fire! If you do not take care, you together with my wax models may catch fire and burn in this world, but if this happens, you will burn also in the next world – in the fires of hell!'

At the age of 81, Marie sculpted her very last figure in wax. It was her own likeness and showed her sitting in her black gown and lace-trimmed bonnet, her eyes glinting behind the little spectacles as they stared determinedly straight ahead. In those days not many ladies lived to her great age. Although her thoughts were still clear, she could feel that her strength was fast failing. She had fits of coughing, made worse by the damp English weather and the sooty, foggy London air.

In 1848 another bloody uprising broke out in Paris; revolutionaries once more took over and barricaded the city and the authorities only regained control after a terrible massacre in the streets. Marie worried about the few friends she still had there, even about her husband François who was still alive but deep in debt as usual.

Even more worryingly, in London her sons had started to quarrel bitterly about small things. Francis was jealous of the older Joseph whom he had always suspected his mother preferred. Sometimes the two refused to speak to one another for days on end, although business still came first, and 1849 they mended their differences long enough to plan a trip to

Paris, hoping to buy up souvenirs of the old days at bargain prices in the aftermath of the recent troubles. They worked briskly and efficiently as always; while Francis arranged to find their father a new apartment and pay half the wages for a housekeeper to take care of him, Joseph found himself negotiating with Sanson, the executioner who had been in charge of the guillotine during the terror. This poor and desperate old man – the same man to whom the villain Dutroy had betrayed Marie all those years ago – was glad to sell them his last mementos; and they carried back to London the blade of the guillotine itself and the executioner's axe.

The grim reminders of sudden death were put into Madame Tussaud's 'Separate Room' – the part of the exhibition that was closed to 'those of a nervous disposition' and off-limits to young children. *Punch* magazine had a better name for the grisly attraction, and a name that stuck; they called it 'The Chamber of Horrors'.

Not long after the boys had settled back into

London life, they heard that their father had died suddenly. He left only a few pieces of furniture and crockery, and there was not one word in his will about the wife whose wealth had supported him for so many years.

Joseph and Francis had inherited their mother's flair for modelling and her head for business, too, and so when Marie became too weak to work and they took over, the waxworks flourished. One day the 89-year-old Madame Tussaud went to her bed unwell, and this time she did not emerge from her chamber. She knew she had not got long to live, and while she could still speak she asked her family and servants to gather round her bed.

On April 15th 1850, as Francis and Joseph bent over, straining to hear her, she announced that they would share her fortune in equal parts. She made them promise solemnly that they would never again quarrel, and told them not to be too saddened, but to thank God that He had allowed their mother to live such a long life. Then Marie's tiny head sank back; her thin hair was as white as the deep pillows and her cheeks and stiffening fingers were just like wax. The old lady's eyes closed for the last time, and her hands lay still on the coverlet.

EPILOGUE

Madame Tussaud had been right to warn her manager about fire. In 1925 a stray spark from the wiring of a great electric organ set the premises on Marylebone Road alight. The buildings were burnt almost to the ground, yet somehow staff managed to carry nearly all the models through the smoke and flames to safety.

Then, more than a decade later, the World War II Blitz by German bombers reduced everything in the surrounding streets to rubble. Where the exhibition's storeroom and the restaurant had stood there was nothing but a huge crater, but by some miracle the main buildings were untouched. King George VI and Queen

Elizabeth, whose wax doubles were on display inside, came to inspect the damage and to show their sympathy.

Madame Tussaud's had long since become a British institution. More than a century on, it was easy to forget how it had all begun, amid the turmoil of the French Revolution. Years after Marie Tussaud's death, there still sat, in the middle of the exhibition, like a family of ghosts, Louis, Marie-Antoinette and their children, and poor Madame Elisabeth. Down on the floor below in the Chamber of Horrors were the masks of the King and Queen's dead faces, staring from glass jars like specimens in a laboratory. Locked away in a hidden cabinet the Princess de Lamballe still smiled faintly.

And just by the entrance sat another ghost, the little old lady in her black bonnet, her long fingers outstretched to receive the coins of the visitors as they jostled to get in...

HOW A WAXWORK
MODEL IS MADE

Marie Grosholtz, later Madame Tussaud, used several
techniques when she made wax portraits or full-size models for
her exhibitions.

If she could work using a living person she would take a mould
of the person's face as quickly as possible, using a thin coating of
plaster. She would cover the face with a paste, leaving very small
holes at the nostrils into which two tubes of tightly rolled-up
paper would be inserted so that the person could breathe for the
ten minutes or so needed for the plaster to set.

The plaster-cast of the face was removed and later, in her
studio, Marie would pour hot melted beeswax (a substance made
by bees for constructing their honeycombs) into it to make a
model of the features, which she could then smooth over and
sculpt using delicate tools.

If she was working with the head of a corpse, Marie could
take her time – except when the executioner or gravedigger was
hurrying her along! In this case, she would use thicker clay to
make the mask, once again filling the hollow mould with wax
later on to get a lifesize and lifelike model.

Sometimes a picture – a fine painting, a simple sketch or a

print torn from a book, perhaps – was all she had to work from, in which case Marie would use a wooden compass and a ruler to make sure that the eyes, nose, mouth and ears were in the right proportions and the correct distance apart from one another.

Natural beeswax is a perfect material to make models in, either when it is warm and soft and can be pulled and pushed into shape with the fingers, or even when it has hardened and a knife has to be used. Later, in England, Marie used a prepared waxy substance, mixed with petroleum jelly and other oils, which was stronger and more flexible still.

The most important part of any wax model was the face, and Marie might spend weeks sculpting to get the features exactly right. For the cheaper exhibits, only the face and hands were made of wax, while the rest of the body was a framework of wires and wooden struts, put together by a craftsman under Marie's supervision and covered with clothes, made or adjusted to fit by a seamstress. (Over the years Marie spent a fortune on fine costumes for her models; some of her subjects were so flattered that they donated their own clothes for the exhibitions.) The most elaborate models were all wax under their clothing – the arms, legs and bodies of which could be modelled by anyone roughly the same size as the subject.

Once she was satisfied that a face (with its ghostly

yellowy-white complexion) was a near-perfect shape, Marie's next job was to give it the colours of a living human being, using almost transparent colours for the skin and finishing off the cheeks and lips with powder and oils. Marie was not merely a mechanical modeller, a pourer of wax and a mixer of paints, but an artist; her genius was in knowing just how to create an expression by a little raising of an eyelid or the corner of a mouth. The hair that Marie used was usually real human hair, and every single one – whether for a head, or the eyebrows and lashes, or a beard, or sideburns – had to be sewn separately into place with a special needle.

The waxwork model's eyes were made of glass, and the teeth of ivory or porcelain (sometimes real teeth were collected from a dentist or, it was rumoured, from the gravedigger, too). These were pressed carefully into position with a little gum to hold them fast.

NOTE: Don't try this at home! Do not consider modelling faces without getting advice from an expert – if it isn't done absolutely correctly it can be very uncomfortable – and dangerous!

TIMELINE

1760 – Anna Maria Grosholtz, the future Madame Tussaud, is born in Strasbourg.

1764 – Anna Maria's mother takes her to Berne, Switzerland, to join the household of Dr Philippe Curtius.

1767 – Anna Maria and her mother follow Curtius ('Uncle Philippe') to Paris where he has established his exhibition of waxworks.

1780 – Anna Maria, now known as 'Marie', is sent to the Palace of Versailles as art tutor to the Royal Family.

May 1789 – Knowing that the Revolution is brewing, Curtius tells Marie to return to Paris at once.

July 1789 – The Paris mob storms the Bastille, signalling the start of the French Revolution.

October 1789 – The King and Queen and their children are taken to Paris and imprisoned in the Tuileries.

1791 – The Royal family try unsuccessfully to flee from France.

1793-1794 – The Terror grips Paris.

April 1793 – King Louis is executed.

October 1793 – Queen Marie-Antoinette is executed.

Spring 1794 – Marie and her mother are briefly

imprisoned in La Force prison where they meet Josephine de Beauharnais, the future wife of Napoleon.

Autumn 1794 – Dr Curtius dies, leaving his businesses, and his debts, to Marie.

1795 – Marie marries François Tussaud.

1798 – Marie's first son, Joseph, is born.

August 1800 – Marie's second son, François, is born.

Winter 1800 – Josephine, now married to Napoleon Bonaparte, arranges for Marie to model the future Emperor.

1802 – Madame Tussaud takes her waxwork exhibition to England.

1803-1834 – Marie and her exhibits tour England, Scotland and Ireland.

1815 – Marie models Napoleon, now the prisoner of the British, again.

1822 – Marie is shipwrecked on her way to Ireland and washed up on the Lancashire coast.

1831 – Marie is caught up in the Bristol Riots, but escapes with her exhibition intact.

1835 – Marie Tussaud opens her first permanent wax museum in London.

1850 – Marie dies on April 15th.

1925 – Madame Tussaud's waxworks is almost destroyed

by an accidental fire.

1940 – German bombs damage the wax museum, which survives yet again.

2003 – Tussaud's now has branches in London, Los Angeles, New York and Amsterdam.

Tony Thorne is a linguist, writer and broadcaster, and has homes in London and Strasbourg, where Madame Tussaud was born. He has written several acclaimed works of non-fiction.

OTHER TITLES IN THE **WHO WAS...** SERIES:

WHO WAS... David Livingstone
The Legendary Explorer
Amanda Mitchison
1-904095-84-4

Born a poor Glasgow cotton-mill worker, David grew up
to become a great explorer and hero of his time.

This is his incredible story. The tough man of Victorian
Britain would stop at nothing in his determination to be
the first white man to explore Africa, even if it meant
dragging his wife and children along with him.

He trekked hundreds of miles through dangerous
territory, braving terrible illness and pain, and was
attacked by cannibals, rampaging lions and killer ants...

WHO WAS... Anne Boleyn
The Queen Who Lost her Head
Laura Beatty
1-904095-78-X

For Anne Boleyn, King Henry VIII threw away his wife, outraged his people, chucked his religion, and drove his best friend to death.

What does it take to drive a King this crazy?
Was she a witch? An enchantress? Whatever she was,
Anne turned Tudor England upside-down and shook it.
And everyone was talking about her...

But Anne lived dangerously. And when she could
not give the King the one thing he wanted – a son –
his love went out like a light. The consequences for Anne
were deadly...

WHO WAS... Alexander Selkirk
Survivor on a Desert Island
Amanda Mitchison
1-904095-79-8

On the beach stood a wild thing waving its arms and hollering. The thing had the shape of a man, but it was all covered in fur, like a Barbary ape. What was it? A new kind of animal? A monster?

It was Alexander Selkirk, Scottish mariner and adventurer, thrilled to be rescued by passing sailors after four years alone on a Pacific island. This is the story of how Selkirk came to be stranded on the island and how he survived, the story of...
THE REAL ROBINSON CRUSOE.

WHO WAS... Ada Lovelace
Computer Wizard of Victorian England
Lucy Lethbridge
1-904095-76-3

Daughter of the famous poet Lord Byron, Ada Lovelace
was a child prodigy. Brilliant at maths, she read numbers
like most people read words.

In 1834 she came to the attention of Charles Babbage, a
scientist and techno0whizz who had just built an amaz-
ing new 'THINKING MACHINE'. Ada and Mr
Babbage made a perfect partnership, which produced the
most important invention of the modern world – THE
COMPUTER!

WINNER OF THE BLUE PETER
BOOK AWARD 2002!

WHO WAS... Charlotte Brontë
The Girl Who Turned her Life into a Book
Kate Hubbard
1-904095-80-1

Of the famous Bronte siblings, Charlotte, the eldest, was the survivor. At eight, she was packed off to a boarding school so harsh that it killed two of her sisters. Her adult years were equally haunted by tragedy.

But one thing kept Charlotte going: she had a secret talent for story-telling. This is the tale of a remarkable woman, who turned her own life into one of the world's greatest classic novels, *Jane Eyre*.

WHO WAS... Ned Kelly
Gangster Hero of the Australian Outback
Charlie Boxer
1-904095-61-5

Born into a family of Irish settlers in Australia, Ned Kelly grew up bad. Cattle and horse thieving led him into regular dust-ups with the law. Then, at 23, while on the run, he shot a policeman dead.

For two years Ned and his gang of outlaws hid in the outback, making a mockery of all attempts to catch them. This is the story of how a bushranger declared war on his country's police and became a great national hero.

WHO WAS... Florence Nightingale
The Lady with the Lamp
Charlotte Moore
1-904095-83-6

Even as a little girl, Florence Nightingale knew
she was different. Unlike the rest of her family, she
wasn't interested in fancy clothes or grand parties.
She knew God wanted her to do something different,
something important... but what?

In 1854, shocking everyone, she set off to help
save the thousands of British soldiers injured in the
disastrous Crimean war. Nothing could have prepared
her for the horror of the army hospital, where
soldiers writhed in agony as rats scuttled around
them on the blood-stained floor.
But Florence set to work, and became the greatest
nurse the world had ever seen...

Dear Reader,

No matter how old you are, good books always leave
you wanting to know more. If you have any questions
you would like to ask the author, **Tony Thorne,** about
Madame Tussaud please write to us at: SHORT BOOKS
15 Highbury Terrace, London N5 1UP.

If you enjoyed this title, then you would probably enjoy
others in the series. Why not click on our website for
more information and see what the teachers are being
told? **www.theshortbookco.com**

All the books in the WHO WAS... series are available
from TBS, Distribution Centre, Colchester Road, Frating
Green, Colchester, Essex CO7 7DW
(Tel: 01206 255800), at £4.99 + P&P.